Lexile:

LSU ☑yes
SJB ☐yes
BL: 4.3
Pts: 0.5

CITY CRITTERS

YOUR NEIGHBOR THE
SQUIRREL

GREG ROZA

WINDMILL
BOOKS ™

New York

Published in 2012 by Windmill Books, LLC
303 Park Avenue South, Suite #1280, New York, NY 10010-3657

First Edition

Editor: Jennifer Way
Layout Design: Greg Tucker

Photo Credits: Cover, pp. 4, 5 (top, bottom), 6, 7, 8, 9, 10, 11, 13 (top, bottom), 14, 15 (bottom), 16, 17 (top), 18, 19 (top, bottom), 20, 21, 22 Shutterstock.com; p. 12 © FLPA/S., D., & K. Maslow/age fotostock; p. 15 (top) Oxford Scientific/Getty Images; p. 17 (bottom) Karen Strolia/Flickr/Getty Images.

Library of Congress Cataloging-in-Publication Data

Roza, Greg.
 Your neighbor the squirrel / by Greg Roza. — 1st ed.
     p. cm. — (City critters)
 Includes index.
 ISBN 978-1-61533-383-7 (library binding) — ISBN 978-1-4488-5123-2 (pbk.) —
ISBN 978-1-4488-5124-9 (6-pack)
 1. Squirrels—Juvenile literature. I. Title.
 QL737.R68R694 2012
 599.36—dc22
                                    2010048303

Manufactured in the United States of America

For more great fiction and nonfiction, go to www.windmillbooks.com

CPSIA Compliance Information: Batch #BS2011WM: For Further Information contact Windmill Books, New York, New York at 1-866-478-0556

CONTENTS

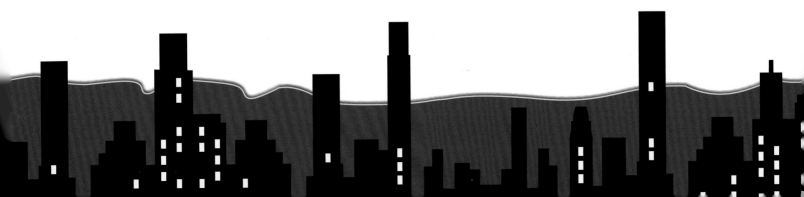

SQUIRRELS IN OUR WORLD

Earth is crawling with wildlife. Animals live just about everywhere on Earth. They live in the deepest oceans and on the tallest mountains. Many animals live far from places where many people live. However, some animals do just fine in towns and cities.

Squirrels live on five of Earth's seven **continents**. You can find tree squirrels

This gray squirrel is looking into a city trash can. City squirrels will eat many different foods left behind by people.

in just about any place that has trees. Although many live in **rural** areas, many others make their homes in **suburbs** and in city parks. You generally do not have to try very hard to find them. Squirrels are not shy!

Top: In the wild, squirrels are known for making nuts a big part of their diets. *Bottom:* You can find squirrels in forests, parks, and backyards.

5

There are more than 230 **species** of squirrels. You are likely most familiar with tree squirrels, such as the gray squirrel, the red squirrel, and the fox squirrel. Squirrels are rodents. Rodents are small, furry **mammals** with four front teeth used for **gnawing**. Depending on

The eastern gray squirrel, shown here, is found throughout the eastern half of the United States.

the species, adult squirrels are between 5 and 36 inches (13–91 cm) long and can weigh between .5 ounce (14 g) and 4 pounds (2 kg).

Unlike many wild animals, squirrels have **adapted** well to living in towns and cities. They are generally very brave around people. Some will even take food out of people's hands.

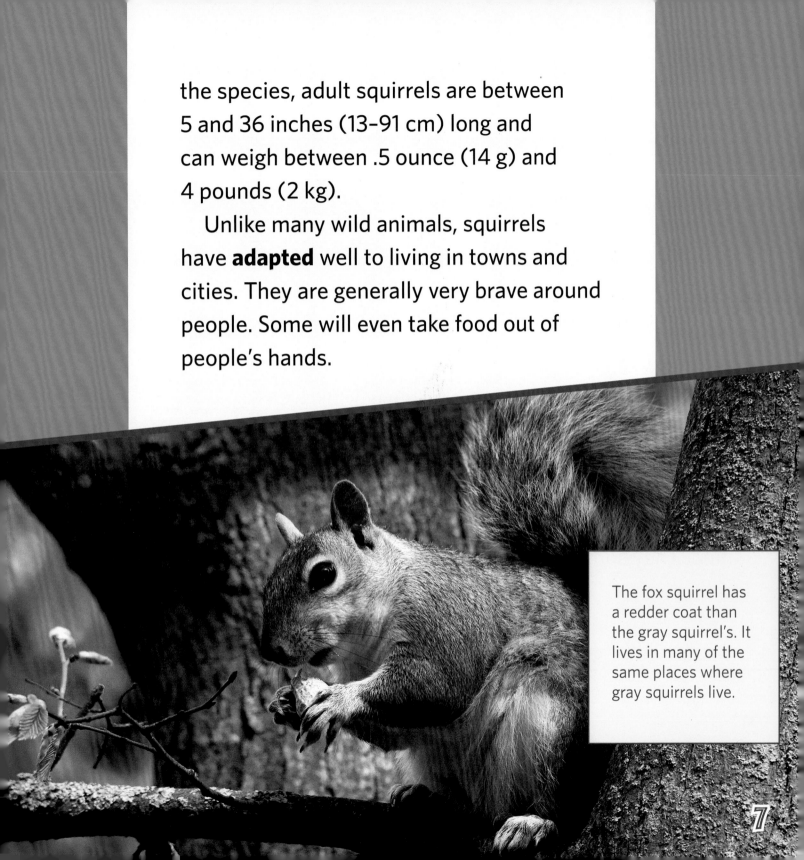

The fox squirrel has a redder coat than the gray squirrel's. It lives in many of the same places where gray squirrels live.

Squirrels are **omnivores**. Most people know that squirrels eat nuts. They also eat seeds, fruit, flowers, bark, and insects. They gnaw on bark to keep their teeth sharp.

Since nuts and seeds are not always plentiful in cities, squirrels often eat whatever they can find. They sometimes

The red squirrel lives throughout Europe and in parts of Asia. This squirrel species has tufts of fur on its ears.

dig through garbage cans for leftover food, such as bread, bones, and even sweet snacks. In suburbs, bird feeders are a common source of food for squirrels. This angers many suburban homeowners!

Squirrels dig in the ground for seeds to eat. They also dig small holes in which to store food.

SQUIRREL MATES

Male and female squirrels of the same species look very similar. Males tend to be slightly larger and heavier, though. Females often live longer than males.

Squirrels are adults and ready to **mate** by the time they are one year old. Adult squirrels generally mate twice a year, once in winter and once in late

Ground squirrels make their homes in the ground instead of in trees.

spring. During mating season, several male squirrels will chase one female squirrel and fight over her. If you live in a city, you might see this chase happening high in the treetops. After the chase ends, the female mates with one of the males.

Here are a male and female squirrel hanging in a tree by their back feet.

SQUIRREL PUPS

Depending on the species, squirrel **gestation** can last from 30 to 60 days. Then the mother gives birth to a litter of babies. Most litters have three or four babies. Baby squirrels are called pups, kits, or kittens. Newborn pups are blind, toothless, and hairless. A pup is about 1 inch (2.5 cm) long and weighs about 1 ounce (28 g).

Here is a mother squirrel in her den with her litter of newborn pups.

Left: Squirrels can get into holes in trees to make their homes there.
Bottom: This is a young male ground squirrel.

The female takes care of the pups alone. The pups can take care of themselves by the time they are 16 weeks old.

Squirrels have life spans of between three and six years, depending on the species. However, most city squirrels die before they reach adulthood because of the constant vehicle traffic.

There are three main kinds of squirrels. They are tree squirrels, ground squirrels, and flying squirrels. Tree squirrels and flying squirrels live where there are lots of trees. Ground squirrels such as prairie dogs generally live away from people. Most of the squirrels that live in urban and suburban areas are tree squirrels.

Here is a squirrel nest, or drey, high up in a tree.

Right: This gray squirrel is building its nest in a tree. *Bottom*: Squirrels can climb down trees headfirst. They can do this because they can turn their back feet so their claws can grip the trees.

Although squirrels generally live alone, they sometimes form small groups. Tree squirrels will nest inside trees, or they will make nests of leaves in high tree branches. Squirrel nests are called **dreys**. Mother squirrels use their own fur to line their nests.

SQUIRRELS IN YOUR NEIGHBORHOOD

North America's eastern gray squirrel has largely displaced the red squirrel in Great Britain.

Squirrels have good memories. They can find their food stores months after they have buried them!

Squirrels love seeds. They will eat all your birdseed if you let them!

Flying squirrels do not really fly. The skin between their front and back legs lets them glide like a kite does.

When you are at the park, look up and you may see one jumping from one tree branch to another.

If you see a small pile of leaves tucked between tree branches, you have likely found a squirrel nest.

Squirrels sometimes run along power lines. If they step in the wrong place, they can be shocked and killed!

CITY DANGER

In the wild, squirrels have many **predators**, including hawks, owls, snakes, and even cats. Young squirrels are at greater risk than adults. Red squirrels can live for up to about six years. Fox squirrels can live about seven years. Eastern gray squirrels can live to be about nine years old.

Cats are good hunters that sometimes catch and kill squirrels.

Squirrels have far fewer enemies in cities. There are other dangers, though. City squirrels are so used to the sounds of cars and trucks on the streets that they often do not see them coming. City squirrels generally live only about one year.

Top: City squirrels are often killed by cars, not predators. *Bottom*: City squirrels tend to live shorter lives than squirrels that live in forests.

SQUIRRELS AND PEOPLE

Many people think squirrels are cute. Others, however, feel they are pests. It is hard to keep squirrels from raiding bird feeders. If one squirrel figures out how to get into a feeder, others watch and copy it.

When tree branches reach over the tops of houses,

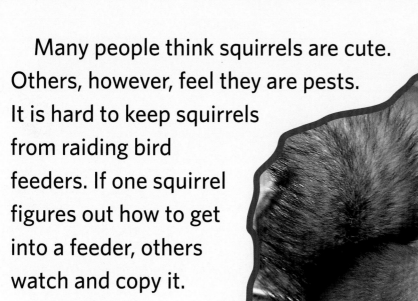

Some city squirrels are so used to people that they eat out of people's hands. Do not hand-feed squirrels, though. They can also bite!

squirrels are known to make nests in attics. Squirrels in attics can cause a lot of damage. They can gnaw wood and shingles, causing the roof to leak. They can also gnaw electrical wires, increasing the risk of house fires. Many urban and suburban businesses specialize in trapping and removing squirrels.

Squirrels may dig up seeds in gardens. This is annoying to gardeners!

SQUIRREL SAFARI

It is generally not hard to find tree squirrels in a city. Although they are less active in winter and when food is scarce, squirrels can often be seen gathering nuts, building nests, or chasing each other. Even when squirrels are not in plain

You might see an eastern gray squirrel with all-black fur like this one. This is known as a melanistic squirrel.

sight, you might see proof that they live nearby. Squirrels use their nests for only a short time. Sometimes they build more than one. You will see wood on which they have sharpened their teeth. You might even find a pile of nuts and seeds in a hole in a tree. Going on an urban squirrel safari is a fun way to learn more about these animals.

GLOSSARY

ADAPTED (uh-DAPT-ed) Changed to fit new conditions.

CONTINENTS (KON-tuh-nents) Earth's seven large landmasses.

DREYS (DRAYZ) Squirrels' nests.

GESTATION (jeh-STAY-shun) The amount of time a baby stays inside its mother.

GNAWING (NAW-ing) Biting things.

MAMMALS (MA-mulz) Warm-blooded animals that have backbones and hair, breathe air, and feed milk to their young.

MATE (MAYT) To come together to make babies.

OMNIVORES (OM-nih-vorz) Animals that eat both plants and animals.

PREDATORS (PREH-duh-terz) Animals that kill other animals for food.

RURAL (RUR-ul) In the country or in a farming area.

SPECIES (SPEE-sheez) One kind of living thing. All people are one species.

SUBURBS (SUH-berbz) Areas of homes and businesses that are near large cities.

INDEX

WEB SITES

For Web resources related to the subject of this book,
go to: www.windmillbooks.com/weblinks
and select this book's title.